Spread The Jam

Spread The Jam

An Essential Guide to Sitting In and Jamming with Musicians

by
Joe Kennedy

Printed in the United States of America
ISBN: 978-0-578-35531-3

To My Mom & Dad
Thank you for the years of jam sessions, support, encouragement, assistance, and guidance. You were instrumental in helping me pursue my passion and follow my dreams. I could not have made it without you. The way you cared for my interests and supported me was significant in my journey. The way Dad would walk in to a bar and convince musicians to let some unknown 17 year old kid join them on stage will always be a mystery.

Thank you. Thank you.

Table of Contents

Acknowledgement

I would like to thank my wife, Tara, for her enduring support, encouragement, and patience. The jams, concerts, gigs, late nights, early flights, celebrations, and noise show no signs of ending soon. Here's to embracing the noise! Thank you Tara.

I must express my sincerest thanks to Pat Hannigan. His guidance, critique, and constructive feedback on editing and revising was instrumental in the development of this book. Thank you Pat.

Thank you Gary Lekas for spotting the potential in me at 15 years old and telling my parents that I should be going to the jam he hosted. Gary also gave me my first music teaching gig at the music store he owned. He provided the space for me to grow, and the environment to nurture the development. Thank you Gary.

Preface

Do you know those jitters you get before riding a rollercoaster? What about the feeling of anticipation when walking through a haunted house? That feeling of not knowing what exactly is going to happen but knowing it will be fun and memorable. That's what it's like to play on stage for many musicians! That's the feeling that charges you up. The rush of dopamine from that oh-so-good feeling that overtakes you when you are playing your ax. That's what I'm talking about!

After reading this book you should be able to take the stage and fire off a killer tune and absolutely nail it. You will have an idea of what to expect, what some of the unknowns will be, how to prepare ahead of time for some of the obstacles you will face, and how to navigate your first time signing up for a jam or playing out with others.

Once you've gone to a jam, written your name and instrument down on the list and are waiting for your turn to play, you likely will feel that nervous energy coursing through your body. Do you sit? Do you stand? Should you check the list? Are you still signed up? Did you spell your name right?

My name is Joe Kennedy, and I cut my teeth playing at jams and sitting in with bands. I was in a band in high school that played a local festival. A member of the sound company at the festival, Gary, heard our set and approached my parents about my playing. He suggested I come to the blues jam he hosted weekly at a local bar. I was 15 going on 16. This was the summer of 1999. My parents checked it out without me and decided to bring me to the bar. I remember early on, Gary would sit under the Hammond organ on stage and work the volume pedal for me because I had never played the organ. I loved it. It was uncomfortable, I didn't know enough, I was nervous, I made mistakes, I messed up songs, I failed and musically fell flat on my face a lot, but I kept coming back. Week after week my parents and I would sit in the same place, right in front of the stage, and I'd listen carefully to all the other guests that would play. When they'd call me up for my two songs I was ready to go. Some of the musicians weren't thrilled about my being there, but others were very helpful, offering tips and constructive criticism after I played. They would tell me songs to learn, what I did well and what I needed to review more. They showed me musical cues and gestures they used and how to interpret them, told me what I could do to improve, and how to interact with the other players on stage. They really helped shape my early musical growth and development. I love the blues. I love playing the blues and still pop into blues jams and sit in.

I attended every jam I could in the area where I lived. I would meet musicians at one jam, they would tell me about another, and the next week I would see them at the new spot. It provided a great networking opportunity and a chance to play with many different musicians.

At 23, I moved to Las Vegas and attended every jam I could to introduce myself to the new scene. I didn't know anyone and none of the musicians had worked with me. It takes time to break into a new scene, so I used my skills from all the jams I had attended to sit in and network with the musicians already playing. It proved beneficial, as I was working around town within 3 months. I moved to New Orleans at 25 and used these same techniques to become an active participant in the professional music scene here.

It is my goal with this book to help you understand the process of sitting in, how to get ready and be prepared when you go, how to make the most of the time you'll have, and to be successful.

This book has accompanying audio recordings and they can be downloaded free of charge at:

https://bigjoekennedy.com/spread-the-jam

Illustrations 1-24, 36, 39, and 40 have recorded examples to accompany the book. Additionally, Illustrations 39 & 40 have been transcribed and the sheet music has been included. The transcriptions can be downloaded in concert, Bb, Eb and bass clef.

Spread The Jam, Volume 1.

Joe Kennedy

Mike Fulton

Ted Long

Mark Weliky

Bryan Besse

Cover Illustration by Sergio Garzon

Chapter 1

The Beginning

So you want to sit in. Great! I learned so much from sitting in with bands and going to open jams. Maybe you have been playing for a while on your own and you are ready to venture out and try some things with other players. That can be done at jams too. There are many different ways you can sit in. Some musicians will have players sit in on their gig. You can attend local open jams or search out artist showcases in a specific genre of music. Each of these types of scenes will offer something different and provide you with great learning opportunities and experiences.

In some instances, you will get something similar from them, and in other ways, they will be different. If a musician is asking you to sit in on their gig that isn't a jam, that is a sign of respect. In many cases, musicians aren't going to let any random person that comes into the club play on their gig. The musician has an agreement with the club to provide entertainment of a certain caliber. To maintain their working relationship with the establishment, they are sometimes less likely to invite an unknown entity up to play.

Open jams are opportunities to network, play, and hone your skills. There are many different kinds of open jams. Some have a house band that backs up jammers, others are more solo/duo settings where each person that signs up plays their stuff for a specified amount of time. There are jams where the house band starts the night off. After their set the jammers are pieced together to make enough instrumentation to form a band for each set. With this type of lineup, you may have never met the other musicians. There is only a short amount of time to figure it out.

There are great takeaways from each experience. A showcase can be invitation-only, or it can have a sign-up. Some showcases have a house band and feature singers or headline entertainers who rotate through and the house band backs them up. Other times, the showcase will feature a specific genre. It may be an acoustic open mic that likely would have acoustic guitars and singers. Other instrumentalists may be welcome, but it would take some investigating to clarify the specifics of the event.

Remember, not all open mics and showcases are right for everyone. Sometimes I would show up at a new open mic to find out it was an acoustic open mic with a PA and a mic stand. That is more geared towards the singer/songwriter style and if I didn't have a keyboard with me there was nothing for me to play.

If I attended a new jam and they were playing a bunch of rock tunes, and I got up to play Afternoon In Paris, or Donna Lee, it would be my mistake for not reading the room appropriately. If I went to a jazz jam where they were playing bebop jazz tunes and called Boom Boom by John Lee Hooker, they could have played it because it's a 12 bar blues, but the material wouldn't align with the theme or style of the jam. It's important to be aware of the atmosphere and repertoire being played.

Music is the language we use to communicate, and for many it is a foreign language. To see musicians who have never played together sit in, be able to say a few short sentences and play something amazing is an art. It is communication across many levels and requires the players to listen attentively to each other. If there are five players on stage, all five have to be attuned to one another. If one player is not listening to and responding to the musical conversation it will show.

This book is geared towards helping you become aware of the vocabulary, the language, and the fundamental building blocks of the music so you can get out there jamming and playing with your friends. If you can play music, you can play with someone who doesn't speak your verbal language by communicating with the notes and expressive interpretations, and by listening to and responding to the other players.

Sitting in with others is one of the best teaching tools because it is a real-world application of the skills that you have been practicing. It offers a chance for reacting to another player and responding to that player's reactions.

Think of it like sparring for a fighter. The fighter trains with the coach, drills moves, rehearses pivots and level changes. When going through the rehearsals they are creating muscle memory and refining their skills. Sparring will put the training to practice. The live opponent will move differently and change angles, creating an unpredictable set of variables for both fighters. For the musician, sitting in is the sparring. We get to listen to other soloists, respond to their playing, and feel what responses our playing generates in others.

In this book we are going to make some assumptions about your knowledge of basic chords, rhythms, intervals, and music theory components. If we discuss something in the following chapters that you are unclear on, clarification and additional explanation no doubt will be readily available on Google. Roman numerals will be used to show chord changes. Capital roman numerals indicate major chords, and lowercase indicate minor chords. I7 is a dominant chord built on the first scale step of the key center. In C, I7 is C7, ii7 is D-7.

Chapter 2

Going to the Jam

Is this your first open jam? Do you have a friend that is encouraging you to sit in on their gig? Are you nervous? Have you played out before? Have you ever played with others? Are you afraid of messing up? These are skills and experiences that will get easier with time. The more you perform in front of people, the more comfortable you will find yourself in the spotlight.

Think about the first time you gave a presentation in front of a class for school. You may have spoken quickly, said "umm" more times than you'd care to count, and stumbled over your words. It's like taking free throws in a basketball game. You practice the shot through repetition, creating muscle memory for the way to cradle the ball, how much force to use when shooting it, the release point when you set the ball free, and the flick of the wrist at the top of the shot. This skill can be practiced. Stage presence and controlling your nerves are similar.

If you are looking at playing in front of an audience for the first time, remember, everyone started there. We were all beginners at one time. Before you go to the jam or to sit in, there are some skills, techniques, and sensations you can work on at home during regular practice, such as singing into a microphone, holding the mic properly, and what to do with your hands if you plan an instrument that rests or are a singer. If you are new to playing with others, it is important to have steady time. This goes for singing and playing. If you are going to be doing both at the same time make sure you assess how fluid you are with transitions and changes while playing with something like a metronome. The stage lights can make it difficult to make out the audience.

To help in creating a good first-time experience for yourself practice the motions and movements you'll be doing. Grab a microphone and mic stand and practice singing into it if you're a singer. It does not have to be plugged in. The focus is to get comfortable with what height you like the mic, and how far away from you or your instrument you want it. To work on your time you can practice with a metronome. To work on playing with a band there are apps like iReal Pro, and the computer program Band-In-A-Box that you can play along with. There are also play-along tracks on YouTube that you can practice with. (Disclaimer – I am not affiliated with any of the programs or websites listed here. I receive nothing by mentioning them.)

There is nothing like the real thing, and these practice tips are helpful, but nothing helps like getting out there and playing with others. You will be nervous. That's ok! You will make mistakes. That's ok too! You will learn, you will grow, you will develop your musical skills and ability to communicate with other musicians.

If you've scoped out the scene and found an open jam or a friend has asked you to sit in on one of their gigs, the next step is to make an appearance. Once you arrive, what do you do? What do you play? Do you bring someone with you? How do you network?

My first recommendation is to attend the gig or open mic without intending to play. Check out the scene. See what tunes they play, how the host operates the show, what the interactions are like between musicians, and try to pay attention to what material they are playing that the audience responds well to.

If you are sitting in on someone else's gig there isn't a sign-up sheet. You'll be performing with the musicians on that gig. You will need your instrument in most cases. When will you not need an instrument? When you play one that will already be at the gig, such as keyboard/organ/piano. If you play drums you will sit in on the drums that the drummer is using already. Bringing yours and setting them up isn't going to happen. Bring your own sticks, though. Some guitar players and bass players will share their instruments with someone sitting in, others will not. That is a personal preference, and everyone feels different about sharing their axes.

In most situations, it is best to bring your own instrument, cables, strap, stand, tuner, and amp. Bring a small to medium-sized amp and leave the slew of effects pedals and looping station at home. At jams, the turnaround time is often kept to a minimum and having excessive gear will take up a lot of space and time. Horn players need to bring their instruments. Brass players will share their instrument on occasion, and some have a sterilization spray they spray the mouthpiece with before and after. Reed players should bring their own horn. Not many players will share a reed instrument.

When attending a new open mic or sitting in with someone, if anything is unclear, asking is always easy. All you have to say is, "Do I need to bring anything?" Call your friend, or the club, or the contact listed as the open mic host. It's a normal question to ask.

Sometimes you will end up sitting in with people you've never met, and it isn't an open jam. Musicians can get away with this if we know how to speak the basic language that will be discussed in the following chapters. Every encounter is different, but there are times you'll meet a band or a group of musicians playing a gig and after a short conversation they ask you to join them on stage for a number or two. How does this happen, and why? Some gigs are welcoming to sit-ins and others are not. When you find yourself talking to musicians on a gig that is welcoming, there are many reasons why they may have asked you to join. Maybe you have a mutual friend. Sometimes you both may have worked the same club or circuit. Others may just be curious to hear you. It is possible they have heard of you. There may be a good salesman pumping you up to them where their interest is jabbed a little. Either way, it is an honor to be invited to share the stage with fellow musicians, and remember that you are a guest.

The only way to meet new musicians when you see them out performing is to introduce yourself. Many players are willing to chat on the set break with people who have come out to support their show. Start by commenting on a tune they played, or some aspect of the performance you enjoyed. If the conversation is reciprocated, they may ask you if you play an instrument. Once you get a conversation going, they might pop the question; "Hey, would you like to play a tune with us?" A few important points for this introductory exchange though. If you're going to ask to sit in, you must respect the answer. Also, going with the flow and groove they have established is recommended. This isn't an opportunity to pick apart the gig. Don't complain about the sound or the tune selections. Be courteous to the audience, remember the band is there to make money, and to make the listeners happy. One tip with sitting in on another musician's gig is to not sit in every time they perform. Some players may even express to you their desire to not have you sit in every time. Be respectful and don't overstay your welcome.

If you are attending an open jam, make sure the music you plan on performing fits the style of the jam you plan on visiting. When you arrive, bring in your instrument. If you want to play, search out the sign-up sheet. It may be located at the front of the stage, or at the bar or with a host. Ask another musician where to sign up if it isn't clear. Some popular jams end up with a full list of players before the event even begins. In those cases, you need to get there before the start time when the sign-up sheet is made available. This will help you get a spot to play, and the extra time before the playing begins can be used to get to know the other players. If you don't know the host or host band, try to have a word with the host(s) of the jam to give them an idea of your level of experience and if there are players you know or would like to play with. Other jams may have the sign-up sheet organized by instrument. This helps form small groups and combos from the people signing up. Each configuration of players may get to play 4-6 songs, hopefully sharing it among the ones who want to sing or be featured.

One important distinction to make clear, an open jam is different from an open mic and an open stage. An open jam is where players gather to make music together. There typically isn't a rehearsal, and combos of players are put together based on who is in attendance. Having whole bands sit in together may or may not be acceptable. It is best to talk with the venue or the host before going to an open jam and looking to play as a band to be sure that type of sitting in is ok. An open stage or open mic is a little different. An open mic is oftentimes just that, a microphone and a pa system at a club, coffee house or other types of performance venue that people can sing, perform spoken word or comedy, and try out material. An open stage is similar to an open mic and provides an opportunity for full bands and other performance combos to perform and try out material.

Now that you are signed up, you need to figure out what to play if you are asked to call a tune or two. It may or may not be up to you, and this can be communicated with the host of the jam. If you do want to call the tunes, generally the goal is to pick the stuff you are most comfortable with, you know the key, and how to explain the whole song to the other players. Explaining the song to others will be covered a little later. What you want to work on before the jam is two different and contrasting songs. Sometimes you'll be asked to play one, other times two. In some situations you'll play 20 or 30 minutes. Even if you want to play all night, it's about showing respect to other jammers and not monopolizing the time. That's why we will use two tunes as our examples. When choosing contrasting songs, some things to think of are; major and minor, faster and slower, swing and straight.

After you get two songs completely memorized where you know the form, melody, lyrics if singing, chord changes, an introduction, how to come in after solos, and an ending; then you're ready to go to an open jam. You will be able to use them for a few visits, but it may get boring playing the same two songs every time. To alleviate this, learn more songs. Unless it's an original composition, players are covering others' songs. If you are at a jam and you hear a song from another jammer, make a note. Look the song up and learn it.

The jam that I started playing at when I was in high school had a reputation of being a great jam in town, and it was also a very supportive place. The host of the jam welcomed kids that could play, but they had to be able to *play*. The state law was that underage people could be in the bar as long as they had a legal parent or guardian with them. There was a young guitar player that would come quite a bit. He and I became friends over the years and have played numerous gigs together. When we were kids we often got paired up to jam together. During this time I was trying to learn more tunes, learning how to sing, and work on my stuff. I liked some of the tunes this guitar player would sing so I learned a few of them too. One night we got paired together and I was calling the first tune. I called the one he often did and sang it first. This friendly rivalry lasted for many years with us playing and singing songs the other performed but doing them first at a jam. It created a friendly "Now what are you going to do?" vibe. Just be careful not to agitate another player, and realize not all musicians will take to this kind of play. They should take it as a sign of respect that they played a tune in a manor that moved you to want to learn it and play it too.

When you are at the jam, signed up, and waiting your turn, there are a few things you can do that will help you and others at the jam. Before you take the stage, tune your instrument if it requires tuning. This will prevent everyone in attendance from having to listen to you tune-up and will help streamline the process of changing over players. As you are waiting for your chance to play, buy things from the establishment. If it is a coffee shop grab a coffee or tea. If it's a club or venue have a drink, and it doesn't have to have alcohol in it. The businesses that are supporting our desire to gather and perform need our support to keep it going. It is important that we understand our role as patrons and performers. If you're attending a jam at a public library drop a fiver in the donation bin you likely passed near an entrance. Be supportive of the people supporting you.

Any time you sit in, whether it is at an open jam or on someone's gig, be kind and enjoy the music being performed. It doesn't help you learn and grow as a musician if you have a "higher than thou" attitude about other players. This isn't a place to compare and criticize, it is a place to complement and collaborate.

Chapter 3

Jam Etiquette and Networking

There are some things you can do that will help you network and play more. Thank the band. You made music with others, thank those players. Thank the host of the jam, or the host band. Thank the venue for supporting live music. If it was packed, the list had more players than ever before on it and you only got to play one song, thank them. Showing gratitude and having a positive outlook can help create opportunities. Make sure you have respect for players of all levels. If you have been playing for 25 years and have been to over 994 jams, be nice to the beginner that just messed up the form because he hasn't played out before. If it's your first time playing out and you just messed up the form, listen to the rest of the band. Hopefully, the 25-year veteran musician is humble, kind, and helpful, and shows you where they are in the form.

If you are setting up your gear or using someone else's be efficient. When it's your turn to play, get on stage and ready to play quickly. Once you have played your tunes, grab your gear and exit the stage quickly so the next group playing can set up. Be aware of your volume and keep balanced with the rest of the group. A nice balance helps everyone hear what's going on. Never put food or drinks on top of amplifiers, speakers and electronics.

You can use your phone and record a voice memo of your set to listen back to. You will be able to hear how effective your communication about the song was. Analyze if everyone knew how to start and end it and if you communicated things in a way they could understand. You will be able to analyze your performance and tend to what needs improvement. Then, 3-6 months down the road you can record yourself and listen to the difference. Ask yourself questions such as: Is your time better? Do the ideas of your solos link together? Are you developing an idea or just playing notes? Are you rushing slow tempos?

The experiences and education you will have after playing at 15 – 25 jams with different players will amaze you. Real-world experience is one he!! of a teacher. You will develop your musicianship, your stage presence, and your communication skills.

Another aspect of playing at jams to appreciate is playing with more advanced players. Many top-level musicians have played at jam sessions and there are times where you can find these experienced players sharing the stage with beginners. Sometimes a veteran player will have such command of the pocket of the piece that you get wrapped up in the groove and feel something memorable. Other times the experienced players will musically change you. The experience of playing with them could push you to pursue your passion. Those moments propel us to keep playing.

At this point, you went out to a jam or to sit in with friends, you signed up if necessary, you picked the songs you wanted to call, you knew how to run down the tune with the players, you played and it went great. What now?

Introduce yourself. Work up the courage to walk the room and converse with other players, and not just the ones you played with. These people are part of a network of individuals that like something you do and already make time in their schedule to participate in it.

12

You should have business cards if you're going to actively gig. This doesn't mean you are going full time, and are planning a tour, but that you are open to working a gig. If someone at the jam likes your playing they may want to play with you more. Your business card should include your name, instrument, and how you can be reached.

Only you will know when you are ready to go to a jam or sit in with other players. Before you're going to go out to sit in, go sneak a peek at one of the jams in your area. Just observe. You will be able to see the repertoire they are playing, how the players are being called up to play, who the leader or host is, and what the other players sound like. You can then decide if you would like to play at that jam. If so, next time bring your instrument. If you feel like you'd want to work up to that jam with some smaller ones first, keep exploring your local scene and find a jam you feel comfortable at. Once you debut you can decide where you want it to take you.

Don't let a lack of experience stop you from getting out there and trying. Everyone was a first-timer at everything in life. That's the only way it works. You don't have to think about using a fork any longer, but there was a time when you had never used one. Every musician had a time before they played out. The jam is a great learning opportunity in a low-stress performance setting where you can play with others.

Most of the people at jams are there to support the scene and enjoy some live music. Occasionally you will run into people who will be critical of you. You will get a cold shoulder, or they will criticize your playing, or they'll avoid playing with you. Some musicians will be threatened by a new face or new talent. They will ignore you. They will not tell you the key, or song structure so you mess up. Don't let these experiences prevent you from continuing to show up though! These things are going to happen. It's part of the way things go. You can only control how you respond to it. The majority of your experiences are going to be positive. You may encounter a jam where it's the culture to be curt to newcomers. It's your call if you want to continue to pursue a musical relationship with those players or venue, or find a setting that is more open to sharing the stage with new players.

The musicians who can see themselves in you will likely be helpful. For some, it will be the tenacity in your determination to get out there and play. It may be the sound you get from your instrument or the lilt to your feel that strikes a chord with the welcoming ones. Also, watch for the quiet players that stay neutral for the first little while. I have had great musical friendships form after a player stayed quiet and just observed my entrance to the scene and we formed a friendship later. The musicians that help are frequently the ones that received help themselves. Someone extended a hand and offered some guidance to them, and they are returning the favor to the next player.

Veteran musicians can hear when things are going off, such as when someone gets lost on the form or forgot the chord changes in the middle of their solo. If you are playing with an experienced musician who is there to support the scene, they will likely have a way of helping you that won't draw a lot of attention to the fact that you're a little off. If the guy on the other side of the stage started yelling, "E FLAT . . . A FLAT. . . G MINOR, C SEVEN . . . NO! C SEVEN!" That may embarrass you. I know it would embarrass me. Have you ever tried to rub your belly and pat your head? If a musician is looking at you and patting the top of their head, they are trying to tell you that they are at the top of the form. They are trying to discretely assist you in getting back on track. If you get lost, look around. Someone will probably be helpful because they've been there.

Chapter 4

Form

The form of a piece can give clues to what's going to happen. If I am sitting in with a group and they call a song I don't know but they feel like I will catch on quickly, I will ask some important questions to give me a feel for what to expect. I'll ask: is it major or minor, what key is it in, and what's the form?

You will encounter many different types of forms, but there are some that come up frequently and it is important to understand them. It's important to know the different blues forms --. the 12 bar blues, 8 bar blues, 16 bar blues, 24 bar blues. Some forms are abbreviated into letter groupings.

The 12 bar blues is sometimes abbreviated as an AAB form. The two A sections are similar with a slight variation, the B section is new material. The 12 bar blues in this way is broken down into three 4 measure groups. The first 4 measures are on the I7 chord. The second 4 measures are based on the IV7 chord but go back to the I7 chord. The third 4 measures start on the V7 chord and resolve to the I7 chord. This is not a common way of explaining a blues. AAB form can be easily identified in the song, *Song For My Father* by Horace Silver. A few frequently used forms using letter abbreviations are AABA, AB, and AB with a tag. This is explained using roman numerals because the chords associated with roman numerals can be applied to any key. Major key blues first, minor blues in parenthesis. Take a look at *Illustration 1*.

Blues Forms - These forms will likely be played at a blues jam.

I7 (i7)	I7 (i7)	I7 (i7)	I7 (i7)
IV7 (iv7)	IV7 (iv7)	I7 (i7)	I7 (i7)
V7	V7	I7 (i7)	I7 (i7)

Illustration 1

The basic blues has many variations that overlap across genres and styles. One very common variation is a quick change. The difference with a quick change blues comes in measure 2 when the IV7, or iv7 in minor is played, instead of the I7, or i7 in minor. Measure 2 is bold to show that that's the only difference in *Illustration 2*. In comparison to the traditional blues form in *Illustration 1*, the quick change has the change in measure 2, but measure 3 & 4 go back to the I7 chord. The IV7 only lasts for the one measure and quickly goes back to the I7. A quick change.

I7 (i7)	**IV7 (iv7)**	I7 (i7)	I7 (i7)
IV7 (iv7)	IV7 (iv7)	I7 (i7)	I7 (i7)
V7	V7	I7 (i7)	I7 (i7)

Illustration 2

Another common variation is in measure 10. In a traditional blues, measures 9 & 10 are both the V7 chord, but it is very common in the blues for measure 9 to be the V7 chord, and measure 10 to be the IV7 chord. This can happen with, or without the quick-change variation. It is something you'll have to learn to listen for. The chord instruments (piano, guitar, organ) and the bassist will be easy to detect if they are changing in measure 10 by going down a whole step or not. So, a blues, with a quick change, and the V7 – IV7 will look like *Illustration 3*.

16

I7 (i7)	IV7 (iv7)	I7 (i7)	I7 (i7)
IV7 (iv7)	IV7 (iv7)	I7 (i7)	I7 (i7)
V7	**IV7 (iv7)**	I7 (i7)	I7 (i7)

Illustration 3

Additionally, adding a V7 chord in the last measure of each chorus is frequently used. Sometimes the whole last measure, other times just the last 2 beats. This is shown in *Illustration 4*. In this example, the quick change is still being used, and the IV7 chord in measure 10 is being used, but they don't all have to be used together. This is something you'll have to practice listening for – and listen to lots of blues songs and forms to develop your ear – so you can hear it once or twice and know what's going on.

I7 (i7)	IV7 (iv7)	I7 (i7)	I7 (i7)
IV7 (iv7)	IV7 (iv7)	I7 (i7)	I7 (i7)
V7	IV7 (iv7)	I7 (i7)	I7 (i7) **V7**

Illustration 4

For analysis, let's look at a couple of blues songs that are frequently called at jams that are different than the variations discussed thus far, but utilize some of the variations discussed.

i7	i7	i7	i7
iv7	iv7	i7	i7
bVI7	**V7**	i7	i7

Illustration 5 – Thrill Is Gone, B.B. King

Thrill Is Gone, Illustration 5, does not use the quick change, nor does it use the V7 chord at the very last measure. Also, B.B. King did something different in measures 9 & 10. In measure 9 he went

17

to the bVI7 chord – the flat-six, dominant 7 chord. This resolves down by a half step to the V7 chord, the dominant chord.

Next take a look at *Illustration 6*, the song *Call It Stormy Monday Blues* by T-Bone Walker. Measure 3 has a bII7, that's a flat two chord. Lower the second scale step a half step and make it a dominant 7 chord. It's resolved by going back down to the I7 chord. Measures 7 & 8 have the diatonic walk up from I7-ii7-I7/III then back to I7. The tune then goes to the V7 like most blues do in measure 9, and finished to the IV7 like a regular blues. Some bands have evolved the tune over the years and added a half step up to the bVI7 in measure 10, then back down to the V7 but not every band plays it that way so use your ears to figure out what way they are playing the last 4 measures. Measure 11 adds in a bII7 chord. This is a lot of changes from the basic blues mentioned earlier. It requires some practice to get it but it's worth it because you can ace it when you go to a jam and this gets called.

I7	IV7	I7 **bII7**	I7	
IV7	IV7	I7 ii7	**I7/iii**	**I7**
V7	**IV7** (**bVI7** **V7**)	I7 **bII7**	I7	(V7)

Illustration 6 – Call It Stormy Monday Blues

I can clearly remember being about 16-17 years old, sitting in the smoky bar playing at the jam and both *Thrill Is Gone* and *Call It Stormy Monday Blues* get called. The bass player was trying to help me out and giving me "the look" and strongly landing on the bVI7. After I totally missed it the first few times he began doing it while adding the emphasis of moving the neck of his bass and doing the additional head nod when going down the half step to the V7. I just didn't know. I would hit the V7 chord each time against the bVI7 and would release the notes and not play anything for a moment because I could hear the crunch being created by my part. It was an uncomfortable feeling. I knew the bass player was trying to help me out. I missed it that night, but the players that were giving me constructive feedback told me after the set what I was missing. With "Stormy Monday" they told me it was a blues with a walk up. As correct as that is, I wasn't too familiar with passing chords, diatonic turnarounds, or substitute turnarounds. I struggled through that tune for a few weeks. You've got to use the resources available to you. YouTube wasn't a thing. Facebook hadn't been invented yet. I couldn't just look them up. I had to find the tracks on a CD at the library and check it out or ask my Uncle Tim who was a huge blues fan and knew most of the players I was sitting in with personally.

Many blues jams play the song *Mustang Sally.* It's a 24 bar blues. Everything is doubled. Take a look at *Illustration 7* to see how everything is twice as long. This song does not use the quick change, but it does go to the V7 chord in the last measure, usually with a rhythmic hit on the & of 1, down beat of 2, and on 3 and the & of 3. There is also a break in measure 19, everyone hits the downbeat together on 1 and rests the rest of the measure and the next measure. The vocal line takes this break during singing, and soloists fill this break during solos.

I7	I7		I7	I7
I7	I7		I7	I7
IV7	IV7		IV7	IV7
I7	I7		I7	I7
V7	V7	bV7	IV7 (HIT on 1)	(BREAK)
I7	I7		I7	V7

Illustration 7 – Mustang Sally

The 8 bar blues is a bit different. It still goes through the I-IV-V chords. In *Illustration 8* you can see that the chord changes come

19

in the same order as the basic 12 bar blues, but the duration is shorter. Also, it is an option to go to the V7 chord at the end of the 8 bar blues just like it is with the 12 bar blues. Sometimes the V7 at the end comes only on beats 3 & 4.

I7	I7	IV7	IV7	I7	V7	I7	I7 (V7)

Illustration 8

There's a variation of the blues where there's a long I7 chord. Sometimes there are hits with band breaks, other times the band plays throughout the form. Most of the time, after the long I7, the rest of the form follows the standard 12 bar blues and it ends up being 16 measures long. The chords and form are shown in *Illustration 9*. An easily identifiable song that uses this is *Jailhouse Rock*. There is a hit on 1 of measure 1, then rests the rest of the measure. Measure 2 has rests for beats 1 & 2, then hits on the & of 3 and holds the rest of measure 2. This is repeated a total of 4 times taking up the first 8 measures, then a shuffle or walking feel the rest of the form. The hits are repeated again for each additional verse of vocals. The hits can sometimes be played in the solos too, but isn't as common. Let your ears be your guide for that part.

I7	I7	I7	I7	I7	I7	I7	I7
IV7	IV7	I7	I7	V7	V7 or IV7	I7	I7 (V7)

Illustration 9

<u>Other Forms</u> - These forms will likely be called at a jazz jam.

There's a form called AABA that has a lot of options or variations, but knowing the basics of it can prove helpful. Let's look at a couple popular AABA songs that have different chord changes. Typically, an AABA song is going to be 32 measures long, and consists of 4 different sections. The A sections are repeated very

20

similarly each time, and the B section is a bridge. Each section is 8 measures long. *Illustration 10* is the song *Five Foot Two* and the song *Honeysuckle Rose* is *Illustration 11*. *Five Foot Two* has what is often referred to as a "rhythm changes bridge." This is a bridge used by popular music of the past and jazz standards based on the bridge to the George Gershwin tune *I Got Rhythm*. Let's look at the jazz form, "Rhythm Changes" based on the Gershwin tune in *Illustration 12*.

The original chord changes to *I Got Rhythm* were a 34 measure tune with a built in turnaround at the end of each chorus. A turnaround is a series of chords that harmonically lead us to either a new section or back to the beginning. In the generic rhythm changes form it's often reduced to a 32 measure form with the tag on the very last chorus if applicable to the melody written over those changes. In this configuration the whole song takes 4 lines. 8 measures per line, 32 measures total. This means each section of our form takes one line on the illustration. There are 4 sections to an AABA form. Two A sections, a B section, and an additional A section. The first two lines are the A sections. Line 3 is the bridge. Line 4 is the repeated A section. When talking about lines in the following examples I am referring to the specific line of the illustration. If an example has chord changes above and below each other in a measure, the upper chord is the first 2 beats, the lower chord is the last 2 beats.

This whole line would be an A section
This whole line would be the second A
This whole line would be the B or Bridge
This whole line would be the final A

I6	III7	VI7	VI7	II7	V7	I	V7
I6	III7	VI7	VI7	II7	V7	I6	I6
III7	III7	VI7	VI7	II7	II7	V7	V7
I6	III7	VI7	VI7	II7	V7	I7	V7

Illustration 10 – Five Foot Two

ii7 V7	ii7 V7	ii7	V7	I6 I6/III	IV7 V7	I6 IV7	iii7 VI7
ii7 V7	ii7 V7	ii7	V7	I6 I6/III	IV7 V7	I6	I6
I7	I7	IV7	IV7	II7	II7	V7	V7
ii7 V7	ii7 V7	ii7	V7	I6 I6/III	IV7 V7	I6 (IV7	iii7 VI7)

Illustration 11 – Honeysuckle Rose

I6 vi7	ii7 V7	iii7 vi7	ii7 V7	I6 I/III	IV7 #IV°7	I7/V VI7	ii6 V7
I6 vi7	ii7 V7	iii7 vi7	ii7 V7	I6 I/III	IV7 #IV°7	I7/V V7	I6
III7	III7	VI7	VI7	II7	II7	V7	V7
I6 vi7	ii7 V7	iii7 vi7	ii7 V7	I6 I/III	IV7 #IV°7	I7/V V7	I6 V7

Illustration 12 – Rhythm Changes

vi7	vi7	vi7	vi7	II7	V7	I6	vii°7 III7
vi7	vi7	vi7	vi7	III7	VII7	III7	V7
I6	I6	I6	I6	II7	II7	II7	V7 III7
vi7	vi7	vi7	vi7	II7	V7	I6	I6

Illustration 13 – Everybody Loves My Baby

22

Illustration 13 starts on the minor six chord. It is the song *Everybody Loves My Baby* and it also follows the AABA format. What you should notice about *Illustration 10-13* is that they are following the same form (AABA) but not the same chord changes. They are very different from each other, but they all use the same 32 bar song structure. It's a form that needs to be internalized and understood so it can be used when sitting in and when analyzing songs you are learning. Take a listen to the playing examples that accompany this book. You'll hear that the sound of the 3 different examples above are all different, but when zooming out and listening to, and analyzing the broader picture, they are identical in their form. There are similarities, and there are hundreds of songs that fit the AABA format.

Compare the audio file for *Illustration 13* to *Illustration 10-12*. The drums were different. On 13 the drummer did a floor tom beat for the A sections and swung the bridge. This is a utilized format in some older jazz tunes and you should know how to play your part to accompany this figure.

Look at the bridge of *Illustration 11 & 13*. This will be the third line of each illustration. The first and second line are the A sections, the third is the bridge, and the fourth line is the repeat of the A section. AABA. The bridge of both pieces start on the I chord, both end up getting to a V7 chord. One of them passes through a minor ii, the other through a major II. These differences need to be memorized specific to each piece because playing a major chord when it should be minor, or vice versa, can clash with the melody and soloist. Also, a trained player will hear this and it will stand out.

AB form is common in older jazz tunes. Songs like *Swing That Music* and *The Curse of an Aching Heart* are both AB form songs. Again, just like with the AABA form, these two AB form songs are very different. Let's take a look. Up first is *The Curse of an Aching Heart* in *Illustration 14. Swing That Music* is *Illustration 15.* Songs using the AB form are frequently 32 measures much like AABA form. There is material that is played identically in both the A section and B section. They differ on the second half of each section.

I	VII7	I	I7	IV	iv	I	I
V7	V7	I	I (VI7)	II7	II7	V7	V7
I	VII7	I	I7	IV	VI7	III7	III7
IV7	i°	I III7	VI7	II7	V7	I	I

Illustration 14 – The Curse of an Aching Heart

I6	I6	IV7	IV7	I6	I6	VI7	VI7
II7	II7	V7	V7	iii7	biii°7	ii7	V7
I6	I6	IV7	IV7	I6	I6	VI7	VI7
ii7	iv	iii7	biii°7	ii7	V7	I6	I6

Illustration 15 – Swing That Music

AB form is easy to identify melodically for some because there is repeated portions that are note for note identical in both the A and B section. In *Illustration 14 & 15* the example is written over 4 lines of chord changes. The first two lines of changes are the A section. The following two lines of chord changes are the B section. Notice if you compare the first line of *Illustration 14* to the third line of *Illustration 14* and the first line of *Illustration 15* to third line of *Illustration 15* they are the same in each tune. It's repeated material that has already been played in the song. Since that material is played twice, these songs could also be analyzed as ABAC. Line 1 is A, line 2 is B, line 3 is A again, line 4 is C. The new material or different material is found in lines 2 and 4. Just like the AABA form songs, these examples are 32 measures long.

24

There is a form that can be classified as AB with a tag, and that covers songs like *Sugar Blues* and other pieces where it's very similar to the AB form, but a small piece at the ending is tagged or a turnaround is added, and this happens every time the song is repeated. Some songs use this technique only on the last time going out as an ending, but songs that have the tagged portion built in every time fall into the category of AB with a tag. Here's *Sugar Blues* in *Illustration 16*. Notice that *Sugar Blues* is 18 measures long. The A section is 8 measures. The B sections is 10 measures because it has the built in tag, or turnaround of the last 2 measures repeated. Comparing this to the AB form, the AB with a tag form follows the style of AB form by repeating material note for note. Measures 1-3 are the same as 9-11. This is the first 3 measures of line 1 and line 2 of the example. The tag that is added to this form is measure 17 & 18. It is the last 2 measures of the B section, measures 15 & 16, repeated once.

I7	I7	V7	V7	V7	V7	I7	I7
I7	I7	v7 I7	IV7	IV7 #iv°7	I7 VI7	ii7 V7	I7 VI7
ii7 V7	I7						

Illustration 16 – Sugar Blues

Another song that uses this extended form is *Ja-Da*. Like the *Sugar Blues*, *Ja-Da* is 18 measures long. Another way to analyze *Ja-Da* is AABA with a tag, because you can break the first 8 measures into two groups of 4, and call them each an A section. This means measures 1-4 is identical to, or very close to identical to, measures 5-8. The B section would be measures 9-12, and the last A section would be measures 13-18, and includes the tag of the last 2 measures. What it means to tag the last 2 measures is, measures 15 & 16 are repeated in 17 & 18. Measure 16 does have a VI7 chord, that is a turnaround chord that leads back to the II7 in measure 17. *Illustration 17.*

I	VI7	II7 V7	I	I	VI7	II7	V7
I biii°7	ii7 V7	I biii°7	ii7 V7	I	VI7	II7 V7	I VI7
II7 V7	I						

Illustration 17 - Ja-Da

Let's analyze this next example.

I	III7	IV	II7	I	III7	IV	II7
I	VI7	I	VI7	I	II	I	VI7
I	III7	IV	II7	I	III7	IV	II7
I	VI7	I	VI7	I	II	I	VI7
I V7	IV	I V7	IV	I V7	IV	bVII	V7
I	III7	IV	II7	I	III7	IV	II7
I	VI7	I	VI7	I	II	I	VI7
I	I	I	VI7	I	I	I	VI7
I	I	I	VI7	I	I	I	VI7

Illustration 18

The piece above is 72 measures long. It can be analyzed in a couple of different ways. In the pop analysis, some might say it has a verse for the first 8 bars, then a chorus for the next 8 bars. This is followed by a second verse for the third 8 bars, and a repeat of the chorus for the fourth 8 bars. The fifth grouping of 8 bars is a bridge. That is followed by a third verse for the next 8 bars, and again a repeat of the chorus for the seventh grouping of 8 bars.

There is a 16 bar vamp or outro on this piece too. Another way to group this piece is to call the verse and chorus together an A section. Then the first two lines of *Illustration 18* is an A section, followed by another A section for the 3rd and 4th line. The 5th line is a bridge, then lines 6 & 7 are the last A section. The vamp or outro then follows. That would make this an AABA form with an outro or vamp or extended ending. This ending doesn't tag specific measures of the piece, it is new material at that point. It has its own melody that is played over that part that is different from the rest of the piece. This song is *Sittin' On The Dock of the Bay* by Otis Redding. Take a listen to the track for *Illustration 18*.

Forms are often cyclical and repetitive. It becomes easier to hear the sections of tunes over time and with practice. Knowing many musical forms is vital to being able to adapt to new material on the spot. The more you know and can identify by hearing it, the quicker you will be able to identify an unknown piece you are playing when sitting in with new players.

Form can influence aspects of the improvisation as well. You can trade measures with another soloist. That will typically be done in groupings that work evenly into the form of the piece. A very common trading setup is trading fours. Each player takes 4 bars or measures and improvises, then shares it with the other players on stage. Here are two ways this can be done. One was is where every player takes a turn with 4 bars and solos. It could go in this order; piano, sax, harmonica, trumpet, trombone, guitar, bass, drums. If it were repeated it would start back with piano and work down the line again. The other way is each player trades 4 bars with the drummer. For example, that way could go piano, drums, sax, drums, harmonica, drums, trumpet, drums, and so on. Everyone trades back and forth with the drummer. This is more frequently the way trading is done. Songs that are a multiple of 4 or 8, like a 12 bar blues, a 32 bar AABA, a 16 bar AB would all work with soloists trading 2's, 4's, 8's or 16's.

Chapter 5

Listening and Communicating

Listening to the other players around you is vital and valuable. Your job is to participate in the piece, add your flavor or voice, and help make the music sound good. You get to add your personality to your performance. One thing you want to do is blend with the ensemble. You do not want to stick out when it is not your turn, because you likely will be interfering with another soloist, a vocalist, or someone playing the melody. It is important that you listen to the others, and if you're the one sitting in with their ensemble, pick up the context clues they are giving you. If everyone gets real quiet all of a sudden, and the vocalist is kind of whispering while singing, you should play softly too. If it's the last chorus, everyone is pumped, the intensity is high, everyone is really going for it, you should be up there with them. Go along for the ride. It should be your goal to blend in and add something, and not detract from the rest of the group.

Make eye contact with the other players. When making music with others, it is important to use your eyes as well as your ears. During the tune you will make brief eye contact with some players, and it could be a brief check-in or just scanning the stage. Other times you may lock eyes with someone and groove together for a moment. It's not you alone up there, you're making music with others, include them in your experience.

An important part of listening is knowing how to listen to a piece and figure out where in the form the musicians are. If you are sitting in at a jam, you may get lost. If it's a blues jam and the band is playing a 12 bar blues, it's important to be able to use clues to help you find your place. The next set of examples will be using blues forms we have talked about previously. You will be shown a form, and will have to listen to the recordings provided with this book to figure out where the band is playing. The recording is going to start somewhere in the form. It is your task to figure out where the beginning of the form is, and where it occurs. It will be played twice on the recording, the second time, the top of the form will be called out.

I7 (i7)	IV7 (iv7)	I7 (i7)	I7 (i7)
IV7 (iv7)	IV7 (iv7)	I7 (i7)	I7 (i7)
V7	IV7 (iv7)	I7 (i7)	I7 (i7) **V7**

Illustration 19

Thrill is Gone – B.B. King

i7	i7	i7	i7
iv7	iv7	i7	i7
bVI7	V7	i7	i7

Illustration 20

I7 (i7)	IV7 (iv7)	I7 (i7)	I7 (i7)
IV7 (iv7)	IV7 (iv7)	I7 (i7)	I7 (i7)
V7	IV7 (iv7)	I7 (i7)	I7 (i7) **V7**

Illustration 21

When dealing with finding your place in the other forms, it is important to be well versed in the form. With an AABA song, if you hear the bridge, that should tell you exactly where you are. For the next few examples, forms other than the blues will be used. Most of the examples will start at the beginning of some section, so the beginning of the second A or the beginning of the bridge, for example.

I6	I6	IV7	IV7	I6	I6	VI7	VI7
II7	II7	V7	V7	iii7	biii°7	ii7	V7
I6	I6	IV7	IV7	I6	I6	VI7	VI7
ii7	IV	iii7	biii°7	ii7	V7	I6	I6

Illustration 22 – Swing That Music

I7	I7	V7	V7	V7	V7	I7	I7
I7	I7	v7 I7	IV7	IV7 #iv°7	I7 VI7	ii7 V7	I7 VI7
ii7 V7	I7						

Illustration 23 – Sugar Blues

I6	III7	VI7	VI7	II7	V7	I	V7
I6	III7	VI7	VI7	II7	V7	I6	I6
III7	III7	VI7	VI7	II7	II7	V7	V7
I6	III7	VI7	VI7	II7	V7	I7	V7

Illustration 24 – Five Foot Two

Knowing forms is vital to being able to sit in. Knowing the basic forms typically found in the style you are hoping to jam in will allow you to pick up on songs and predict with some accuracy what's coming. Knowing the feel of measure groupings is important as well.

What do groupings of 4 measures feel like at 180 beats per minute? How do you know where the beginning is, and when it's coming back again? Where in the form are we? These things take time to develop but put in your favorite blues or jazz track, play some rock if that's what you are into. While you are doing this, listen to the songs. Is there a bridge? Do the verse and chorus occur at repeated intervals? Is there a refrain part that's repeated numerous times? If it's a song you have the music for, or can find the sheet music for, watch the sheet music as you listen to the recording.

Listen closely at the ending of sections or phrases. Do the musicians do anything different with their dynamics, intensity, space? Are they playing more than they were just before? Have they left more silence, or space between things when coming up on the very end before starting over at the top? All these questions are context clues that are often available if you know what to look for.

These characteristics also can assist you in picking out where you are in the music. Listen to many artists. See if there is a common thread that runs among them or if they all do something different. On a specific tune, does everyone play a specific rhythmic hit or the same dynamic level? What about chord changes? Do they get changed? Be aware, they all do something. Think of a poker match. Each player has a tell when they have a good hand or a bad hand. You are watching for this nonverbal communication to make the best decision for your investment in the hand. Think of that when playing music too. Each player is going to have some tells. Drummers often will fill leading up to the beginning of a new section. Chordal instruments may play more leading up to the start of a new section and then leave space, others might leave space towards the end of a section and play more just as a new section is beginning. Horn players may fill improvisations around and between vocal lines. Other times, the horn might be the melody of the piece and playing the lead part.

Instrument roles

Drums are a rhythmic instrument in these settings. They are often not tuned throughout the gig to get different key centers out of the toms or bass drum like a timpani, and the cymbal overtones aren't usually examined on a per tune basis. The drummer lays down a steady tempo and comps behind the melody, the soloist, or the hits of the ensemble. The primary job of the drummer is to keep the pulse consistent and to be the intensity and energy of the group. The drummer sets the feel of the piece.

Bass is primarily a single note instrument. It can play double stops but in these styles, it isn't the primary purpose. Its primary purpose is to play the bass notes, often the roots of the chords and strong chord tones on strong beats. Think of beats 1 & 3 as the fundamental notes and beats 2 & 4 as the passing notes. This isn't always true. An example would be a walking line in C that went C-D-E-G-F. The F was the downbeat of the next measure. Beat 1 & 3 were C & E, the root and 3rd of the C chord. Beat 2 was a D, a passing note making for a smooth walking line. G was a chord tone on beat 4. The bass is the foundation of the groove. The bass part can also be covered by a tuba or sousaphone.

Guitar is a single note, and chordal instrument. It plays comping backgrounds and can play featured melodies. Its primary job is to play chords if another player is playing the melody. These melodies and backgrounds can be improvised or written. The guitar part can also be covered by a banjo or other strummed string instruments.

Piano/Organ is a single note, and chordal instrument. Its primary job is to play chords if another player is playing the melody. It plays comping backgrounds and can play featured melodies. These melodies and backgrounds can be improvised or written.

Harmonica is a single note, and chordal instrument. It plays comping backgrounds and can play featured melodies. These melodies and backgrounds can be improvised or written.

Brass are single note instruments that play melodies and background figures. The melodies and backgrounds can be written in music notation or improvised. Multiple brass players can play together forming chords and harmonies that support the chord changes. These include trumpet, trombone, cornet, flugelhorn, baritone and other members of the brass family.

Woodwinds are single note instruments that play melodies and background figures. The melodies and backgrounds can be written in music notation or improvised. Multiple woodwind players can play together forming chords and harmonies that support the chord changes. These include saxophones, clarinet, flute, oboe, bassoon, and others.

Voice is a single note instrument that sings melodies and background figures. The melodies and backgrounds can be written in music notation or improvised.

It's important to know the roles of the instrument you play and have an idea of the roles of the rest of the ensemble.

Non-Verbal Signals

Listening to the people you're performing with can offer a lot of context clues. There are many nonverbal cues that we can give as musicians. Some are hand signals, some are audio signals, and some are even raising your eyebrows, bobbing your head, or hunching over. Often times when sitting in or going to a jam there will not be music to look at. You are relying on your current knowledge base and listening skills to pick up the piece being played. When sitting in, musicians will often give the key signature with hand signs.

This is another reason to make eye contact with the other players. The nonverbal communication would be missed on you if your eyes were closed, your head was down, and you were taking your own voyage. It's great to lose yourself in the music, but you have to be able to come back around.

If you ever get lost or are unsure of where you are in the form watch the other players that have shown they will help you. If a musician is patting the top of their head they are trying to tell you that it is the top of the form.

Take a look at *Illustration 25*. The hand signals are pointing up. Sharps raise notes. The number of fingers pointing up tells us how many sharps are in the key signature. 1# in G major, 2#'s in D major, 3#'s in A major, 4#'s in E major and 5#'s in B major. Remember though, every major key has a relative minor. 3#'s could also be F# minor. That is why it's important to ask if the tune is in a major key or minor key.

Illustration 25

The same thing can be done for flat keys. *Illustration 26* has the fingers pointing down. These indicate the number of flats in a key signature. 1b is F major or D minor, 2b's is Bb major or G minor, 3b's is Eb major or C minor, 4b's is Ab major or F minor, and 5b's is Db major, or Bb minor.

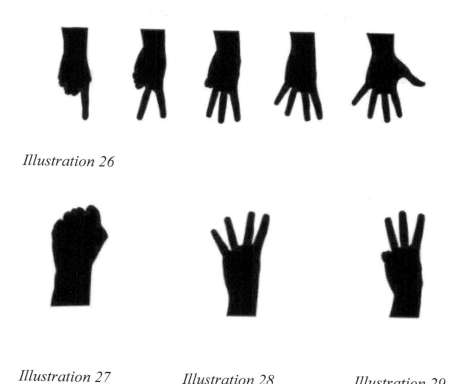

Illustration 26

Illustration 27

Ending

Illustration 28

4 Measures

Illustration 29

8 Measures

The signal for ending a song is often a fist held in the air in *Illustration 27*. In *Illustration 28 & 29* these hand signals can occur near the ending of the piece. If the leader or musical director gives four fingers to the drummer in a jazz band, that often means that the drummer is going to play a four-measure break. During this time the rest of the band might get three fingers like *Illustration 29*. What this means, is for the ensemble or group to play the last eight measures as a tagged ending. If it's the beginning of the piece, and you are given the key you are in, then given the hand signal of three fingers, that can also be a signal to start with the last eight measures as an intro.

If I am going to sit in with a group I have never performed with, I'll give them as much information upfront as possible so we have the highest probability of success. If it's a blues jam and I'm going to play piano and sing, I might say something like; "Blues in Eb, medium shuffle, long I, no quick change, break just before the IV chord." That tells them the key, the feel, the fact that the song hangs on the I chord longer than normal, it has a break before going to the IV chord, no quick change of I-IV-I in the first three measures. All that is left is to count it off and play it down.

Audio signals can be things like playing slightly more attack on 2-3 notes in a row to get your attention drawn to the direction the chords are going, or if there is a ritardando, a solo cadenza or band breaks coming up. This can be done by various members of the ensemble. If you are jamming with a group and someone is offering you help and giving you some nonverbal clues during the song to help you out, pay attention to them. They are trying to help you succeed. Other times you'll hear the bassist or drummer play one loud accent before becoming much softer for a section, causing you to take notice and pay attention. If you are a vocalist sitting in, a guitarist or keyboard player may give you some melody quotes or fragments in the intro to help you be sure your entrance is in the proper key. You may also receive this after a long break or numerous solo sections as a hint that your entrance is coming up, but don't always rely on that. You should be counting along with the rest of the group, keeping your place in the song. The bobbing of the head is oftentimes showing rhythmic hits and you'll hit on the downward motion of the head. This can often be accompanied by raised eyebrows and a look around to get everyone's attention leading up to the head bobs so everyone can be together. You may even hear someone shout out "Hey!" just before a hit or the ending so everyone is listening to each other.

Aside from listening, it's important to understand your function. If you are sitting in, sometimes you will be the featured act for a song or two, and other times you will be a supporting musician joining the rest of the group for a couple of numbers. Knowing your place in each setting can be very helpful in not overstepping any boundaries, overplaying, or upstaging other performers. If it is a jam, most people are there to try things out, play with others, and make some music happen. Pass the solos around, let players who want a ride, take one. If it is a showcase there is probably a list of performers or ensembles. Some showcases are for solo or duo acts; others are geared towards full bands. It is important to know the type of event you are attending so you know if it is the right setting for you. Other times, you may be out and know some musicians who are performing. If they are your friends or musical acquaintances, they may ask you to sit in with them on an instrument or voice. It is up to you to accept or decline this invitation.

Many factors play a role in deciding if you are going to sit in. Is there common material between you and the group/performer? Do you have your ax/horn/instrument with you or will you use one of the instruments from someone on stage? If you are sitting in as a featured artist for a couple of songs, you likely will be able to select songs you are strong with. In this role, you are the star. It's your time to shine and play some of your best stuff. If you are sitting in with the rest of the ensemble, you will likely be playing whatever song they choose. You probably will get a solo but the hang with the other players and the joy of interacting musically with the others will be the focus. One approach in this setting is not to play too much as to detract from the ensemble performance. The goal is to blend in, support the group's musical message and make the music better. It is best in these instances to be complementary to the music and cooperate with the other players. Some say it's best to "stay in your lane until you're invited out of it."

It is good to know what type of sitting in you will be doing, and every time you sit in, it will be different. In order to try to figure out on your own what type of setting it is, ask yourself a few questions. Has anyone else sat in since I've been here watching? If so, were they featured, or were they part of the whole group performance? Is this an open jam, an invitation only jam, a showcase, is it someones gig? If it's an open jam, is there a sign up sheet? If there is a sign up sheet, take a look at it to see if it is set up by instrument grouping, or if people are listing their name and instrument. A lot of this information is available to you by paying attention to your surroundings, and asking the leader of the band, or the host of the jam any questions you may have.

Chapter 6

Many sub-genres of music will likely be covered at any jam you go to. In this chapter, it is the goal to make sense of these sub-genres and provide some idea of what may be appropriate for some of the categories. This list is not intended to be a comprehensive list exhausting all possibilities, but a list to show how to be prepared and adaptable. There is some crossover material and you will likely find musicians who can play many of the styles we will discuss.

Blues

Boogie Woogie: a danceable style often associated with the piano, and repetitive left hand figure or bass figure. Albert Ammons, Meade Lux Lewis, Willie "The Lion" Smith.

Chicago Blues: an electric blues sound, often including electric guitar and harmonica run through an amplifier. Howlin' Wolf, Koko Taylor, Buddy Guy.

Delta Blues: a style from the delta of the Mississippi River area. Style uses guitar, slide guitar and harmonica. Robert Johnson, Muddy Waters, Charlie Patton.

Texas Blues: Single string accompaniment and jazz-like improvisations. Notable artists include Albert King, T-Bone Walker, Big Mama Thornton, Lead Belly, and Stevie Ray Vaughn.

West Coast Blues: This style was a melding of Texas Blues players relocating to California. The style had a prominent piano and jazz influenced improvisations, as well as influence from the high energy jump blues style.
Lowell Fulson, Charles Brown, T-Bone Walker.

Blues Rock: Electric blues style created when artists were replicating the electric blues sounds of Chicago blues and other styles. Think of artists like ZZ Top, Allman Brothers, The Rolling Stones

Jazz Blues: The blues is used in jazz as a song form. The complexity of the 12 bar blues chord changes can vary from subtle turnarounds to cyclic turnarounds going through many superimposed key centers.

Gospel Blues: Blues with a holy theme, or in some cases, a blues musician who became devout and changed their ways.

Jump Blues: high intensity blues, up tempo, usually including a saxophone. Jump blues was revitalized in the 1990's with artists like Brian Setzer and Cherry Poppin' Daddies.

New Orleans Blues: Frequently includes piano and saxophones, pulls elements of jazz and Caribbean influences, piano lead bands included Professor Longhair and James Booker.

Jazz

Traditional Jazz: typically uses a front line of 3 horns. Trombone, trumpet and clarinet. Some pieces are rag form, some are AABA, or AB. Artists like Louis Armstrong, Jelly Roll Morton, Bix Beiderbecke, and Joe "King" Oliver.

Straight Ahead: Typically stated to be the style that took place between bebop and the Herbie Hancock and Wayne Shorter developments. The straight ahead and bebop material is most commonly called at jam sessions.

Bebop: Developed in the early 1940's, into the 50's. It was focused on small group playing, faster tempos, harmonically, rhythmically and melodically more complex than swing style. Cedar Walton, Woody Shaw, Phil Woods.

Hard Bop: This term covers a few different jazz derivatives. It can be associated with a continuation of the Bebop style, a bop based style that uses gospel and blues harmonies and simple repetitive accompaniment, and a very hard driving style with a foundation in bop but the chord structures of compositions aren't based on pop songs of the day. It's a little simplified when compared to bop. It has less chords and more emphasis on the hard swinging feel. Horace Silver, Charles Mingus, Art Blakey, Cannonball Adderley.

Free Jazz: It doesn't follow set chord changes or structures. There is more variance in pitch and texture of sounds produced by an instrumentalist. Ornette Coleman, Sun Ra, Eric Dolphy, Pharaoh Sanders.

Many Straight Ahead, Bebop, and Hard Bop tunes come from what's called "The Great American Songbook." It's a collection of songs from the early 20th century that were composed for Hollywood film, Broadway musicals, and musical theater. Many of the pieces were written between the 1920's and 1960's. They have remained popular in the repertoire of musicians, and endured the test of time.

Rock/Pop

Hard Rock: distortion, heavy aggressive vocals, can be seen as a development past electric blues.

Top 40: This term generically refers to music that is in the top 40 list of most popular songs at that time. The pop/rock genre covers a lot of material and this will be a diverse list of songs.

Classic Rock: This is currently rock music that was a hit between the 1960's and 90's. It is a group of songs that had commercial success.

Being well versed in musical styles is important. It's also important to be able to listen and adapt. If I don't know what a Texas shuffle is, but a guy I'm sitting in with calls one, I will have to look for key markers to help me establish the right things to play. When I think of a Texas shuffle, I think of a swing 8th note, no quick change, 12 bar blues, medium, to medium-up tempo. When someone calls a slow blues, it isn't always clear if they are going to be playing a 12/8 triplet feel, or a slow quarter note 4/4 feel. Asking the person calling the tune isn't always an option. If you are a chordal player, sometimes you have to play a held chord on the first measure to feel out what the rhythm is going to be, and that is often set by the drummer. Then you can jump in with the appropriate accompaniment. If you are a horn player, you can just wait for a measure or two and listen to the groove and enter with a fill leading to the next chord change or section of the piece. *The Thrill Is Gone (Illustration 5)* is often kept in 4/4, while *Call It Stormy Monday Blues (Illustration 6)* often has a 12/8 groove. Both pieces can be classified as a slow blues.

In a jazz jam, or sitting in with a jazz group, the style of a piece can sometimes be assumed if it is a standard that is often played the same way. Other times, the way the group wants to play a tune will be called out before it's begun. If a group is playing an AABA form piece, sometimes the bridge will be played in an opposing style. If the A sections are swung, the bridge could be done in a straight 8th style; or vice versa. *Caravan* comes to mind for this type of tune. The A sections are straight 8th and the bridge is swung. This arrangement is the default way the tune is played.

Sometimes a band will play a song exactly like a definitive recording of a specific artist. For example, the intro to *Autumn Leaves* on the Miles Davis and Cannonball Adderley recording on *Somethin' Else*, (1958).

If an older standard is called that has a verse, make sure to know definitively if the verse is being played or not. If you are going to play the verse it is often good to find out if you will start with the verse or not. What if this was what you were told? "Play a chorus up front, then the verse, then the chorus again. Solos over the chorus chord changes and go back to the verse after solos, then the chorus twice out." That seems like a lot to take in, and right now you probably can't remember the order of verses and choruses. Let's take it again.

In this example we will start with the chorus. This will be the 16 or 32 bar part that many people identify as the actual tune. Then we'll play the verse. Think of the verse as the setup to the chorus. It could provide backstory about the lyrics or story of the chorus. It was often different from the chorus in feel, time, tempo or texture. Then we'll play the chorus again. Now we've gotten to solos and we said solos will be over the chorus. Once the last soloist wraps up we go back to the verse. Once through and it's on to the chorus. This time the chorus will be repeated making for a total of two times through. On that second time through it will likely increase in volume, and be rhythmically and melodically busier.

A tag ending wasn't specified so we're going to assume we will end on beats 3 or 4. This means to end tightly on beat 3 or 4 of the very last measure. If the melody does not play that long it can be improvised over to fill the space but nothing, and I mean nobody, plays past beat 3. Or beat 4. This is intentionally unclear. You won't know exactly how to end it. You'll feel it. There's a certain feeling that takes place that notifies your body how to react and you get to tune in to these tells of our own. Earlier in the book we compared an idea to poker tells (pg. 31). Your body, your mind, your ears, whatever you want to describe it as, will give you tells. It'll take some intuition and you will have had to listen to older traditional jazz albums to pick up this ending. Once you get it, it's easy to anticipate.

There is also a surprise audible that can be called to end a tune with no specified tag. It is called a double ending. This is where the last two measures are repeated right away. No stop, no fills, no drum break. Immediately play the last two measures again, improvising up to beat 3 of the second measure and pop it, or accent it. Or beat 4. Play it with a little more presence. This ending isn't always specified and I admittedly fell flat on my face the first time I was sitting in with a band and they played this type of ending without calling it. It is only two measures long. I ended on a hard 3 like I thought we were going to. Something was clued by a member of the band because everyone else was still playing. I realized we had not ended like I thought. By the time I jumped in the rest of the band was stopping. I got about 2 beats in playing by myself and stopped but it was clear I was not familiar with that ending or however it was cued during the tune.

A tune that comes to mind for that arrangement is the *Limehouse Blues*. This information can be given before the start of the tune, short and sweet, like this. "Ok, Limehouse Blues in Ab. We'll do a chorus upfront, then verse and chorus, blow over the chorus, then go back to the verse after solos, twice through the chorus and out, no tag."

With styles, it is important to know some key characteristics to be familiar with, and able to adapt to what you are hearing. Take a look at the list of the stylistic differences between *Route 66* and *The Thrill Is Gone*. Both songs are 12 bar blues format, but provide an example of stylistic differences. Knowing what is appropriate to play for a specific style is an important skill to develop. It takes a good bit of listening to expose your musical bank to enough material to pull ideas from.

Route 66 is a swing/shuffle	Thrill is Gone is straight 8th
Route 66 has a quick change	Thrill is Gone has no quick change
Route 66 is often played medium to medium/up	Thrill is Gone is often played as a slow blues
Route 66 is in a major key	Thrill is Gone is in a minor key

Illustration 30

When you're new to a jam or sitting in, you can get a lot of tips from watching people play. If a band is playing a song you don't know, analyze the things we talked about above. What's the tonality, is it major or minor? What's the tempo? What's the feel, is it straight or swing? Is there a lot going on or is it more open and sparse? What is the form? Listen to what the other people playing your instrument are doing.

Styles can differ greatly by location. The type of music that will be played at a jazz jam in New York City is very different than the music that will be played at an acoustic jam in Louisville, Kentucky. It is important to know something about the style that is prominent in that region. There are Irish Percussion jams in Southeastern Wisconsin, and you can find Traditional Jazz in Utah. Seek out a setting that suits your interests. Not all styles work well at all open mic and sit-in settings. Know the details about a jam or open mic you will be attending when possible. What type of jam or open mic is it?

If you're going to a blues jam in Chicago, you know there'll be some Buddy Guy and some Junior Wells songs and you'd better know the lick to *Messing With The Kid* and *Sweet Home Chicago.*

If you're attending an acoustic open mic in Nashville it may be original music of various Americana and Country/Pop/Bluegrass styles. Checking out a jazz jam in New York City you can assume to play some standards, some from the Great American Songbook, swing, bop, modern, some pieces will be instrumental and others may have a vocalist.

Most jams and open mics are centered around a certain style or genre of music. Some information can be gathered by the title. An acoustic jam or acoustic open mic is likely going to be guitar or similarly stringed instrument like banjo, mandolin, or ukulele; and vocals. An acoustic open jam will often have solo, duo performances. It can range from all original music to cover songs. A jazz jam will likely cover a broad spectrum of jazz styles, from bebop to Latin jazz, sultry ballads and hot jazz. There will likely be a house band that will play a set before opening it up and having players sit in. There are also jams of improvised music in jazz and the jam band genre. No music is used and the performance is unique and freely spontaneous.

A blues jam is going to include all styles of blues, and sometimes classic R&B, like *My Girl* and *Use Me* or *Sitting On The Dock of the Bay*. There probably will be a house band that plays a bit before opening it up for sit-ins. Some blues jams go into the blues-rock category and incorporate classic rock as well. Showing up to a blues jam and asking to sit in and play *Donna Lee* likely will not happen. You can find a jam that can cover both styles of music, but it isn't appropriate in all cases.

Keep in mind, not all jams and open mics are going to be right for everyone or every style. There were times I'd go to a new open mic and not sit in. Sometimes I was intimidated. The players were really good and I wouldn't want to mess up in front of all those people. Other times, the material they were doing wasn't familiar to me, or the style they were playing was unfamiliar. Over time I would overcome the fear. If I was intimidated, I'd go back again and sign up for the jam the next time. I wanted to know more. I wanted to get to know those players and to be able to make music with them. I was willing to risk messing up or making a mistake to get better. Being challenged musically is important for learning and making progress. It's good to get out there and play, take risks, and see what happens.

I recall one jam I went to and I knew a few of the musicians. The house band brought me up. We played maybe half of the first tune. I must have been doing things wrong that they didn't like because they stopped the tune and thanked me for playing with them. I was asked to sit down. My time was done. I was temporarily crushed by this, but it didn't stop me from continuing to go sit in at other jams. I must have been about 17 at the time. A few years, and many hours of practice later I went to a jam lead by the same house band. They loved my playing and encouraged me to come back. Over time I worked in to the rotation of their featured performers for their weekly jam. I learned a lot from those players. Some of them were encouraging, and others weren't. I don't hold a grudge or ill feelings about any of them. They did what they had to do to protect their gig and maintain the quality they saw fit for their jam. Do I think there were other ways to handle it? Certainly. But, there was also a lot more for me to learn. To receive that kind of eye opening experience at a young age gave me the ability to know what it felt like to be ushered off stage and reduced my fear of having it happen again. Also, I knew what it felt like to fall flat on my face in front of a crowd. I lived. I learned. I came back and played again.

Ideally, you want to have a bag of tricks in a variety of styles so you can adapt to many musical situations. If you are in the house band and the person sitting in calls a tune like *Joy Spring* you have to have some experience with or understanding of that piece. With modern technology, if you don't know the piece and want to read a lead sheet there are many great apps developed that can provide the sheet music and/or chord changes. At the time of writing this book apps such as iReal Pro and Musicnotes are very popular. It helps to have a few variations to the styles you know as well. If you play a chordal instrument, know a few different ways to voice chords, or have a few rhythmic patterns used for comping or grooving. For melodic instruments, know that the fills you play behind a vocalist singing a ballad are going to be very different from the fills behind the soloist on a jump blues tune. Have some variations to your fills in as many styles as possible. For bass and drums, make sure you are comfortable at many tempos with these styles and have a pocket full of ways to walk, swing, shuffle, 2 beat, play behind a soloist or vocalist, and more of the similar. Vocalists should know how to explain the song. They should know the key, approximate tempo through a count off, how to give an intro and outro during a performance or how to talk about it before hand.

Chapter 7

Calling A Tune

You've gone to a jam. You signed up on the list. They called you up. You have tuned your instrument. It's all systems go. Now you have to tell the other musicians what you want to play. So, what do you say? How are they going to understand what you're talking about? Will they know how to start the song? How will the rest of the musicians know the song is over? Not every player wants to be the leader calling the tunes, but if you do, here are some tips.

There is an order of operations and questions to self assess how you need to explain the piece to the people you will be playing with. To simulate calling a tune, the song *Everybody Loves My Baby* will be used to answer these questions.

What is the title of the piece? Tell the title to the players you are sitting in with. (Everybody Loves My Baby)

What key will you be playing this piece in? Is it major or minor? Tell the key and major/minor to the players. (D minor)

Is there a verse? If no, great, move on, nothing needs to be said about a verse at all. If yes, will you be playing it? If no, great, move on, say "No verse" to the players after you've told them the title of the piece you are calling. If yes, will you be playing the verse first, or playing the chorus, then the verse, followed by the chorus. The answer to this will need to be told to the musicians. (There is a verse for this tune but we will not be playing it, so we say "No verse.")

What's the form of the piece you are calling? Is it a blues? A few typical intros or ways to start a song in the blues form are a) take one up front b) from the V c) vamp on the I. When you start with "take one up front" that is telling the horns, or if no horns, the chordal instruments, to play a chorus of the form and the vocalist, or melody player will come in on the next one. Taking it "from the V" is starting on the V chord, and resolving to the I as it does at the end of the blues form. The vocalist or melody player will come in on the top of the form.

"Vamping" can be done with a turnaround, a single chord, a couple of chords back and forth, or various other short repeating patterns. The vocalist or melody player will come in and that will start the top of the form. Sometimes there will be an iconic vamp for a specific song. Those will prove important to know, and if you nail it with confidence without overpowering the band or trying to be the loudest to prove you know it, it'll make you feel good.

Is it an AABA tune? Some common intros for those types of pieces are:
a) last A section b) start at the bridge (the B in the AABA form) c) last 4 measures d) vamp e) take one up front

How to start a song

Starting with taking the "last A section" is just that easy. Start at the beginning of the last A, and the vocalist or melody player will come in on the top of the form. "Start at the bridge" is starting halfway through the form, at the B in the AABA form. The vocalist or melody player will come in at the top. Starting with the "last 4 measures" is just as it sounds as well, play the last 4, the vocalist or melody player will take it at the top. Usually when starting from the last A, the last 4, or from the bridge the melody will be played by some instrument. This helps set everything up. If there's a vocalist they get to hear the melody in the key they will be singing in. Sometimes the band will take the intro with more energy than they will be playing with when the top of the form comes along. This dynamic change from intro to the top of the piece creates an identifiable difference and gives the audience a clue that something is changing. Other times the intro will start quietly and build up to the top. You have to be paying attention to how things start. Be willing to adapt and play with the other players on stage. "Vamping" is used the same here as before, it can be done with a turnaround, a single chord, a couple of chords back and forth, or various other short repeating patterns. The vocalist or melody player will come in and that will start the top of the form. Again, "take one up front" means the same here as before, play a chorus of the form and the vocalist or melody player will come on on the next one.

The way you have practiced this piece should include a way to start it. Be sure to tell the musicians how the piece will start. (We'll start with the last A section and I'll come in singing on the top)

At this point, we could start the tune with the band. They have been told; "*Everybody Loves My Baby* in D minor, no verse, start on the last A and I'll sing on the top." If there are horn players, someone will play the last A section melody, or sometimes they will improvise over the chord changes of the last A. If there are no horn players, it's on the chordal players to improvise something or play the melody for that section. The improvisations in the intros often will be based around the melody and not new thematic material, but that isn't always the case. That's the beauty of this type of performance. You can do something different every time.

If you are calling the tune, you will likely be the one counting it off to start. When you get up to play, your nerves may be going, you may be getting excited to play with a specific player or for someone in the audience. There will be lots of things going on and sometimes a tune can get counted off too fast. Be aware of this and practice counting off the band at a comfortable tempo. One trick I have used for years is to think of a specific melody part or lyric that I know feels right at a specific groove or tempo. Hum the melody or lyric at that speed and then from that tempo count off the band. This is far more common than you may be thinking. I'd like to stress to you that it does happen, even to seasoned veteran performers. It's something we all find ways to overcome with different techniques and reminders for ourselves.

During The Song

After the piece gets going, if you are leading that particular song, look around at the other players. Make eye contact and ask them if they want to solo. Many people are sitting in and attending jams to improvise and play with other musicians. Sometimes everyone on stage will take a solo. Other times players may pass. It comes down to a few reasons to play a solo. How comfortable are you with the material you will be soloing over? Do you know all the chord changes? It also depends on the amount of time left in the gig or that set, the number of players signed up to sit in, how many people are on stage, and many other factors. Sometimes the person calling or leading the tune will solo first, other times they will solo last. Sometimes this will be communicated before hand, other times you will have to use your eyes and ears to pay attention to any clues that may be given out. Did the person leading the song look at any particular player and give them a nod or gesture? Did the singing stop, and no-one came in with a solo so there's just dead space now? If you are very new to the jam scene, use this experience to watch and see how the rest of the players navigate it. Over time you will get used to the amount of time or space that feels natural as "leaving space" before jumping in to take your turn.

Another art to the solos during a song is to try not to have back to back solos from the same instrument type. If there are two guitarists put a different instrument solo between the two guitar solos if both players will be taking a solo. If there are 3 Alto sax players sitting in, try not to have all 3 Alto players solo in a row.

52

The separation can be good for the listeners and the ensemble to remain engaged and present with the tune.

Personally, if I am in the house band, I will not solo on every tune. I'm there to play, to support the other players, to facilitate other musicians sitting in, jamming with others, trying new material, and just having fun. If I am sitting in somewhere, I will likely take a solo on the two, maybe three, songs I play. If there is a house band with piano, bass, drums, and one horn, a guitar player sitting in, and 3 more horn players standing off to the side of the stage all playing along, that's 8 people. If every guy took a solo on every tune there wouldn't be many tunes played per set, and not as many people would be able to rotate in and jam. Additionally, with solos, keep your solos around two choruses or two times through the form of the piece in general. When I was jamming at blues jams the most common solo length was 2x through the form. In a jazz setting this guideline has some flexibility. If you're new to a jam listen to what the other players are doing. If everyone is taking lengthy multiple chorus solos, you could too. My personal experience in the New Orleans Traditional Jazz scene has been that many players will sometimes only take 1 chorus if it's a 32 measure form or one of the variations of those forms. They get in, say what they want to say, and pass it on. With more people soloing, if everyone took long solos the tune would take a long time to play. To help everyone get a chance to play, be mindful of how many choruses you are playing. Being thoughtful and considerate of the other players is important and can lead to being asked back.

Restatement of the Melody

When coming back in with the melody or singing after the solos you have a couple options. If it's a blues form song with multiple verses, come in on one of the verses. At that point, it is up to you. Are there 3 verses and you sang the first two before the solos started? Come in on the top of the form after solos singing that third verse. That'll be perfect! Is it an AABA form song? You can start on the very top of the form or you can come in on the bridge. Coming in on the bridge can be done for various reasons, such as; being short on time, losing the audience, sharing the stage with others, and much more. If you are going to come in at the top, no instructions to the rest of the players are needed. If you want to come in at the bridge, you'll need to notify the others. You can do that with a few different gestures or verbally say "bridge" to the rest of the players.

The hand signals I've seen to let players know to go to the bridge aren't always the same, but they get the message across. I've seen people touch the bridge of their nose two or three times while looking around at the band. Other times I've seen players use their cupped hand with palm facing down moving forward and backward, see *Illustration 31*, that means to play the bridge. I will often use a hand signal along with verbally saying "bridge" to the band as I'm coming back in so we are all together. In a jam setting or sitting in with a group, the material isn't extensively rehearsed and the small call out to go to the bridge isn't going to detract from the performance or the good time of the players involved.

Illustration 31

Take a listen to the track *Hesitation Blues* in the accompanying audio. At 2:00 I tell the band "I got one more" meaning I was going to sing another verse before solos. At 5:33 I say "Take it one time" meaning that we are going to play one more chorus, and the horn is going to play the melody and fills and then we'll end it. If there was no horn or other player to play the melody I would have said "one more" or "one more time" and I would have played the melody and filled. In an unrehearsed gig or sitting in with others these types of hints and clues become part of the tune and performance.

We have figured out how to call a tune, how to give the band some important info, how to count the tune off, what to do about solos, and how to come back in after solos. It's time to end the tune. In some instances it is possible to discuss an ending before beginning the tune, other times the ending will have to be communicated in the middle of a performance. This is ok, and it can be done. Don't worry.

Ending a song

For ending a song, is there an ending the original artist did that is very distinct? Is there a cover of the tune or a version by a specific artist whose style you are emulating? Listen to a lot of versions of a piece. How does each group end the song? Be sure you know some typical endings like the ascending blues walk up, 1, 3, 4, #4, 5678, 1. The descending blues walk down, 1, b7, 6, b6, 5432, 1. Sometimes players will just shout "tag it" and that means to tag the last two or the last four measures, or the last turnaround and repeat it. Typically it'll be tagged, or repeated, 3 times, ending on the third repeat. Another tagged ending for a blues is to repeat measures 9 and 10, the V7 chord and the IV7 chord. Those two measures can be repeated three times, then continue with measures 11 and 12 of the blues form and end with one of the blues ascending or descending licks. Hand signals help cue endings too. Remember these hand signals from earlier?

Illustration 32	*Illustration 33*	*Illustration 34*
Ending	4 Measures	8 Measures

Illustration 32-34 are hand signals used to show an ending is coming up, and what you'd like to do about it. These were also discussed in Chapter 5, page 35, *Illustration 27-29.* The fist held up (*Illustration 32*) tells the other players this is the ending. It is often held up as the end is coming, giving warning to the players that the piece will be ending shortly. It is not intended to be held up the moment you'd like them to stop. Maybe the last 8 measures, or the last 4 measures, depending on how fast the piece is moving. The four fingers (*Illustration 33*) have a couple of uses. It signifies four measures of something. If the four fingers are held up to just the drummer and it is the last pass at the form and the piece is coming to an end, this means for the drummer to play a four-measure solo/fill. During this time the person calling the tune will give the rest of the band a clue. This can be four fingers again. That tells the band to play the last four measures of the piece as the ending. Another option is three fingers (*Illustration 34*). This usually implies to play the last 8 measures as the ending. Some people will hold any three fingers up, others will hold up the middle, ring, and pinkie fingers to show the last 8. Once you understand what the person means, you can identify their intent by their gestures.

The pieces that work easiest with endings of the last four or eight measures are usually AABA and AB form songs. Remember though, there is an AABA with tag, and AB with tag. These are forms with a tag already included, and it's usually the last two measures repeated. There are a couple of options for ending a piece like this. The easiest ending is to simply play the tune as written and end on the last chord and melody note. You can pop it if the melody ends near the last beat of the last measure by stopping on a strong accented note and chord hit, add a ritardando, or hold the last note/chord with a fermata. If someone cued the drummer to play a four-bar fill you have to come back in and play something. When this happens, you have two choices. You can play the last 6 measures including the written in tag in the form and end with one of the ways we just discussed, or you can start at the last 6 measures and only play 4 measures. Leave out the final two measures which are likely a tag of the previous 2 measures.

Another common hand gesture you can use during an ending is the index finger pointed up and moving in a circle. See *Illustration 35*. This means to repeat the turnaround or tag the last few measures, usually two or four measures, usually repeated three times. This gets easier with experience and ways to navigate endings will become second nature. Have a simple plan on how to end the piece you called and know how to communicate that to the other players.

Illustration 35

If you are calling the songs, sitting in or playing at a jam is a place to have fun and play something you are comfortable with that won't require a lengthy explanation. Call something that fits the repertoire that is being played. Pay attention to what the audience is responding to. Are they clapping for bass solos? Are they talking over the ballad, but really digging the mid-tempo grinding shuffle? Keep that in mind when it's your time.

If you are going to play at a jam, or sit in with a band and you are not going to call the tunes, you need to look to the host, the leader, or the vocalist. In some cases, the vocalist will be calling the tunes and leading the band. This person will give out the song title, the key to play it in, the style to play the piece in, count off the piece and lead the ending. This is all the information we recently discussed on how to give the musicians the info about the piece. Everyone's experience level at a jam is different and you need to be flexible. I have played with many vocalists who don't know the key of the song they'd like to sing. They know approximately where they are comfortable singing the melody and usually hum some in my ear so I can find the pitches they are singing, and deduce the key the piece should be in from there. It is not the time to ridicule them for their lack of music theory knowledge or make them feel insecure or unwelcome. Roll with the punches and navigate it in a way where everyone works together and achieves the best end result.

Playing at a jam is an opportunity to learn from others, hear what others are playing, meet the musicians in the local scene, network, hopefully book a gig or two and have a good time. Don't expect perfection. The musicians at a jam are there to play music and support fellow musicians. It is a community and we want to encourage other players and enrich the scene. When you are playing, listen to the other players. Did the drummer just play a certain rhythm behind the chorus that matched a lyric? If you feel like it's going to happen again, catch that hit the next time around and watch the drummer light up that you were paying attention to your surroundings and responding to what the rest of the band was playing. You don't want to be off in your own world.

Another thing you don't want to do is copy every rhythmic or motivic idea. That can detract from the music in no time. It's a skill that requires practice. Some licks and motives are played intentionally to get a specific response from the band. Some quotes get a reaction from the audience. If you recognize a rhythm, pattern or quote from another player, be cautious of playing it back at the musician playing it or copying them. If there is a repeating rhythm or melodic part, emphasizing it isn't always what the soloist wants. Give them the space to develop and be supportive of that. Take a listen to the track for *Illustration 36*. We all tried to copy the soloist. It was too much. There's no space between what the soloist plays, and what all of us are trying to answer with. The music can't breathe. The soloist can't develop their own idea because we are completely in the way. Each player was trying to be the one showing how hip they were.

Illustration 36

When it's your time to solo, that's your chance to show off. If it is a long form, sometimes each player gets one solo through the form. If it's a shorter form, like a blues, each player will usually get two times through the form per solo. This is often referred to as a chorus. A soloist will take 2 choruses and pass it on. Remember to play what you know. You will sound best and most confident and comfortable playing things you know. When it's not your solo be aware of the rest of the group. Don't play over the vocals or fill too much when someone is singing or on top of someone else's solo. Always remember, you are a member of the band on stage. Support the song, play your part, and leave space for others to play theirs too.

Chapter 8

Improvising a Solo

Improvisation in music is the act of spontaneous creation of something melodic, rhythmic, and/or harmonic. It is found in music, art, dance, speech, comedy, rap, spoken word, and much more. A conversation is an improvisation. There is not a script you are following. Hopefully you are listening to the things the other person is saying, and responding to them with your own input. The same occurs at jams. Everyone will take a solo and add their own musical part to the song. Most often, solos are made up on the spot. Sometimes a musician will transcribe a solo from another artist on a specific tune or form and play that as their solo. This is done for a variety of reasons, including to learn the style of a player you admire, to train your ears for aural dictation, or to better understand the musical vocabulary used in the style you play or want to learn. These transcriptions aren't often played on gigs, but the material is used for generating ideas, and developing them.

Every chord has scales that relate to it. Some chords have specific scales that are the best harmonic accompaniment for a specific chord, and other chords have many options for scales to choose from for an improvised solo. When there are many options, you don't have to pick only one. You can borrow from many.

Let's look at a couple of examples. Starting with a chord that will have a very specific scale that is the best harmonic match is C7#11. The best scale to accompany that chord in a solo would be the Lydian Dominant scale, a Mixolydian scale with a #4. Take a look at *Illustration 37*. The top set of keys shows the notes in the Lydian dominant, or Lydian Mixolydian, scale. The bottom set of keys shows the notes in the C7#11 chord. When selecting a scale to play over a given chord you want to pick a scale that reflects the notes of the chord. If we analyze the notes of a C7#11 it's a C major triad, C-E-G, a dominant 7 (also called a minor 7 because it's a minor 7th above the root of C) Bb, the 9th, D, the #11, F#. Technically the 11th is the same note as the 4th but it is called the 11th because we are also playing the 7th. Once you include the 7th you have to call the intervals what they are past the octave. What that means is you have to measure the interval in relation to being higher than the 7th. This is getting into some theory and you can find a plethora of information about chord extensions and I do recommend understanding that further. So, our notes if put in scale form of the C7#11 chord are C, D, E, F#, G, Bb. The C lydian dominant scale is C, D, E, F#, G, A, Bb, C. It includes all the notes of the chord plus an A. The A would be the 13 of a C7 chord and harmonically doesn't clash with the notes we are playing in the chord. All the notes of the chord are reflected in the scale. This is what we're going for with our scale choices in relationship to the chords we are playing. This is how we will derive our choices for improvisations.

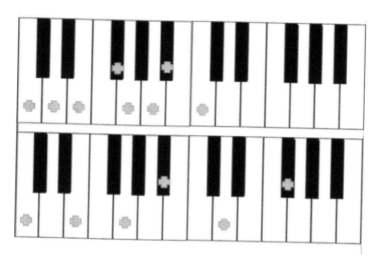

Illustration 37

In *Illustration 38* the top set of keys show the notes of a C7 chord. The second set of keys shows a C major pentatonic scale. The third set of keys shows a C Mixolydian scale. The fourth set of keys shows a C blues scale. The fifth set of keys shows an A blues scale.

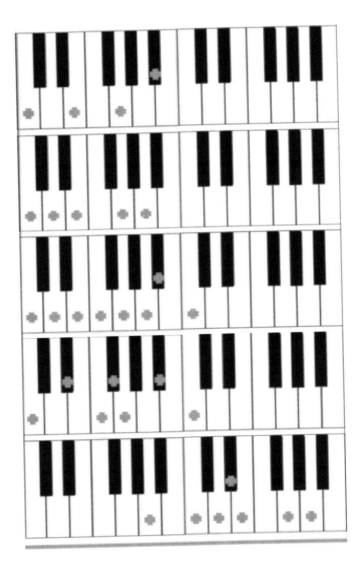

Illustration 38

When looking at *Illustration 38*, the chord C7 has many scales to choose from when improvising. There are more than just the four listed here. The top set of keys is the C7 chord, C, E, G, Bb. The second set of keys is the C major pentatonic scale. Penta is a Greek prefix meaning 5, think pentagram. It's a 5 sided shape. The pentatonic scale is using 5 notes of the major scale. The major pentatonic scale is built using the 1st, 2nd, 3rd, 5th, and 6th scale steps in a major key. This scale can be used on most major triad chords that don't have altered extensions like b9 or #5. This works because it doesn't have notes that are outside the harmonies implied by the chord. It doesn't have a b3 or natural 7. The Bb, or b7, isn't reflected in this scale but it is acceptable to use this scale because it doesn't play a B natural which would create a clash and create dissonance. There are certainly ways to use and resolve a B on a C7 chord, but that's for a more elaborate improvisation conversation. At this point we want to focus on the notes used in scales being reflected in the chords. The major pentatonic scale has the 1, 3 & 5, plus the 2 & 6. The 2 & 6 can also be called the 9 & 13 if they are being played over a C7 chord. This pattern can be applied to any major key center. If you know the major scale, the major pentatonic scale would be the 1, 2, 3, 5, 6. D major pentatonic is D, E, F#, A, B.

The third set of keys is the Mixolydian scale. This scale can be analyzed in a couple of ways. It can be analyzed as a major scale with a b7. It can also be analyzed as the 5th mode major, meaning it is a major scale that starts and stops on the 5th scale step. Analyzing it this way you will understand that C Mixolydian is the 5th mode of the F major scale. C is the 5th scale step in F major, and F has 1 flat, Bb. F, G, A, Bb, C, D, E, F. Therefore, the 5th mode major scale starts on the 5th scale step of a major scale and plays the same notes. C, D, E, F, G, A, Bb, C. C Mixolydian is C, D, E, F, G, A, Bb, C. The chord of C7 is outlined in the scale by assessing every other note. C, E, G, Bb. It fits perfectly into the construct of reflecting the chord in the scale.

The fourth set of keys is the C blues scale. This is a minor scale that is very similar to the minor pentatonic scale, but the blues scale adds 1 additional note. The blues scale is 1, b3, 4, #4, 5, b7. In C this is C, Eb, F, F#, G, Bb, C. The minor pentatonic is 1, b3, 4, 5, b7. The C minor pentatonic scale is C, Eb, F, G, Bb, C. The difference between the minor pentatonic and the blues scale is the blues scale has a passing tone between 4 & 5. The #4 or b5. You can use the minor pentatonic or the blues scale. This scale does have a b3 when the chord has a natural 3. That is ok. This scale will not always be your best choice to play for an entire improvisation but to utilize some aspects of it or use some of the harmonies to create tension and release it with another scale is possible. The #4/b5 is a passing tone and is a tritone away from the root so it will be a tension note, usually to resolve up or down by a half step.

The fifth set of keys is the A blues scale. A is the relative minor key to C major. Remember, that means the notes to A minor are the same as the notes to C major. Now, a dominant 7 chord built on C will not be harmonious with all the notes of the A minor scale, but the A blues scale leaves out the clashing notes. Just like the blues scale built on C, it is built on the scale steps 1, b3, 4, #4, 5, b7, 1. Starting on A, it is A, C, D, Eb, E, G, A. Let's think about the A minor pentatonic scale once. The minor pentatonic is 1, b3, 4, 5, b7. In A that is A, C, D, E, G. The C major pentatonic scale is C, D, E, G, A. Compare A minor pentatonic to C major pentatonic. They are identical. By using the blues scale of the relative minor it includes the b3 and natural 3 of the home key.

What do you do with this information? How do you choose which scale to use? That's the beauty of improvisation. It gets to reflect your personal style, your taste, your own flavor. You aren't stuck with only using one scale for a solo or piece of music. You're free to mix and match scales, borrow notes from one when playing another, play fragments from many of them and figure out what your voice is.

You can start out with C mixolydian and play C, Bb, A, G, then use 2 notes from the blues scale, F ,Eb, then use notes from the major pentatonic and blues scale together and play E, F, F#, G, Gb, F, E, C. Rhythmically, try this playing the first 2 notes as quarter notes, the next 4 as 8th notes, E, F, F# and G, Gb, F as 2 groups of 8th note triplets, finishing with E and C as 8th notes. All of these notes are found in the list of scales we covered above. We did not just stick with one scale, but used fragments of all of them to create a sound of our own. Also, these scales won't all work with an F7 chord or a G7 chord unless you change all the scales to that new key. Generically, over a dominant 7 chord you can use major pentatonic, blues, mixolydian, relative minor blues. There are many other options to include and those options change if there are extensions with alterations. If a chord has a b9, playing the natural 9 will be a clash, so your scale choice will have to reflect this b9. This is often referred to as following the changes. A scale for a b9 chord could be the half/whole diminished, but knowing if it's major or minor would influence our decisions. Context is key. The scales you play reflect the chord they are being played over.

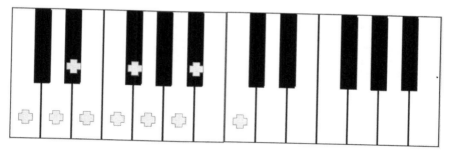

Illustration 39

Illustration 39 is a combination of all the scales from *Illustration 38*. Take a listen to the track that accompanies *Illustration 39*. I play some examples of using only one scale over a given chord, and then use pieces and fragments of the scales and link them together to form ideas out of all the possible notes.

Illustration 39 & 40 Bb, Eb, and Bass Clef can be downloaded at
https://bigjoekennedy.com/spread-the-jam#accompaniment

ILLUSTRATION 39

67

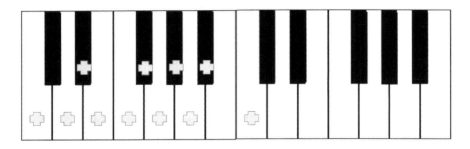

Illustration 40

If you add the chromatic passing tone of the #5/b6 it gives you the possible notes for improvisation as shown in *Illustration 40*. The only notes that are left out are the half step above and half step below the I, or tonic, in this case, C. It's almost the complete chromatic scale. There are ways to use all of these notes in creating an improvisation. Some are more dissonant than others, and some that lead your ear to certain resolutions, but they can all be used on a C7 chord when creating a solo.

There are common improvisation techniques or tricks used to create the basis of a solo. Yes, it is spontaneous composing, you are hopefully playing something original and authentic each time. But in order to learn the vocabulary there are a set of tools.

Motivic Development is taking a specific pattern or motif and repeating it, or using the same melodic and intervallic relationship but starting on different steps of the scale or in different keys or chords altogether. Repeating ideas and intervals, and if they are moved, keeping the intervalic relationships the same. A motif is a short musical idea or statement.

Arpeggiation, or playing arpeggios, means to play the notes of the chord up or down individually. The notes aren't played together like a chord creating harmony, they are broken up like a melodic line.

68

To play **scalar** means to play the notes of the scale in stepwise motion like playing the scale.

Surround tones or enclosures are tricks used when aiming for a specific note. It is playing a half step above and below a note before resolving to the desired note.

Passing tones are when you play a note that isn't a chord tone. It is the note played between two chord tones, passing from one to the other.

Chromaticism is playing notes outside of the key signature or mode of the piece.

Planing, some refer to it as side-stepping, means moving everything up or down a half step. Everything shifts either up or down, or both. Think of Jailhouse Rock. The opening strum-strummmmmmmmmm of the guitar is planing. The chord is kept the same but shifts up a half step.

There are other devices used for improvisation, but this will give us a starting point and a number of examples to show with the track accompanying *Illustration 40*.

This amount of possibilities may seem overwhelming, but fear not! Not all the notes have to be used all the time. Certain notes and scale choices can influence the feel and direction of the solo. You don't have to eat everything at the buffet to enjoy the buffet.

ILLUSTRATION 40

Illustration 39 & 40 Bb, Eb, and Bass Clef can be downloaded at
https://bigjoekennedy.com/spread-the-jam#accompaniment

71

ILLUSTRATION 40

ILLUSTRATION 40

7:03 PLANING/SIDE STEPPING/SIDE SLIPPING

7:19 CHROMATIC LICKS & PATTERNS

C MIN   C#MIN   D MIN   E♭MIN   E MIN   F MIN

ILLUSTRATION 40

(7:36) CHROMATIC TRITONE

(8:03) TRITONE DEMO

74

ILLUSTRATION 40

ILLUSTRATION 40

ILLUSTRATION 40

ILLUSTRATION 40

78

ILLUSTRATION 40

(10:22) PASSING TONES

CT = CHORD TONE, PT = PASSING TONE, CPT = CHROMATIC PASSING TONE

79

ILLUSTRATION 40

ILLUSTRATION 40

81

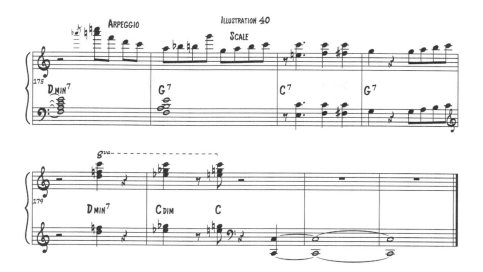

Chapter 9

Tips and Ad-Libs

While this book isn't about the art of improvising, I will propose a few topics to keep in mind. The amount of time you are playing in comparison to how much time you are resting is important. There are going to be times when you are really synced up with the band, you are crushing your solo, the band is blazing, and you are laying down a fire hose worth of notes that are flowing non-stop from you! That'll be amazing. There will also be times when you are playing a soft song, medium ballad tempo, and you are taking the time to develop an idea or a theme. That will be amazing too.

The skill of playing versus resting takes practice. To force the idea into your practicing, play for a specific number of measures, and rest for a specific number of measures. Start with an easy form like a 12 bar blues. Play 4 measures, rest 4 measures. Once you have internalized the way it feels to play like that, and you are making strong lines and creative ideas, switch it up. Try 2 measures of playing and 2 measures of resting. Once you can play relaxed with 2 measure fragments, try 3 measures of playing and 3 resting. You can also play around with playing 1 measure and resting 1 measure.

After you've spent some time practicing the playing and resting, try odder playing and resting combinations. Maybe 5 measures playing, 7 measures resting. Or 3 and 2; 8 and 4; 2 and 6; 1 and 4. There are lots of combinations to try when practicing.

The way this practice will show up in your playing is by leaving space. Let an idea develop. Allow the listener to take in and digest the theme you just played. Take a breath. Take this example for instance. The length of melodies matters. Repetitive things can become monotonous. Over time you see it. You can feel something off. You may not know yet. You're heating up, aren't you? The last 7 sentences have all had five words in them. If your improvisations have the same phrase length all the time it can feel like this to the listener.

Compare leaving space in music to a conversation. A conversation is an interchange of thoughts or information. To interchange is to take turns or alternate. A lecture is where one person is speaking and all others are listening. A lecture would be if a soloist never stopped playing to allow the other musicians performing to react to what was played. We do want the attention of the audience and for them to be actively engaged in listening to our performance. It is important as a soloist that we allow the musicians we are playing with to converse with us too. This is different than trading with another soloist. The conversation is where you leave space for the other musicians playing to respond to something you have played. It isn't a chance for them to start their own solo, but react to what you played, and possibly influence you to play something based on their reaction. It's the back and forth, the musical conversation.

Relate this to someone explaining something or telling you a story. They will make a statement, and pause briefly for you to confirm you understood or ask a question to clarify, or simply say "uh-huh" and then they resume talking. The same can be said for a soloist. They will make a statement, and take a breath. Then they may say 4-5 statements before pausing again, the band may take that pause as an opportunity to react to what was played with a hit, or a turnaround, or something to show they are engaged and responding to the soloist.

Another idea to keep in mind is to develop thematic material. Another way of saying this is to build off of a motif. Doing this can also help you leave space and have a good balance of playing versus resting. It all works together. A motif is a recurring musical idea or subject. To develop these motifs you have to leave space so you can differentiate where one idea ends and another begins. This is what was being talked about in Chapter 8.

Just for fun, read this.
BaBaduBaduBaduBabaduBadadababadababababadabadabada. The lack of spaces forces you to not separate these into phrases. If you leave space though, you can pick up on the intended phrasing a bit better. Check it out.

Ba   Ba   duBa duBa duBabada
Bada   dababa dabababa   dabadabada

There isn't pitch, or meter here. The spacing seen on the page is similar to how you would leave space to develop the idea. Without space, it isn't noticeable to the listener that you are developing something. With space, an idea can stand on its own. The development of the idea can be perceived by the listener. Give the other players time to respond and give the audience time to hear it and process it.

Chapter 10

Wrapping Up

Take note of who is helpful when you are just starting out. Is there someone offering you tips, or constructive criticism of your set? Take it all with a grain of salt. In the beginning, it's important to reflect on a lot of the things other jammers may say, good and bad. You have to figure out some things through trial and error, other times you need an experienced player's mentorship. Some players will scoff at you and the errors you will make in the beginning. Others will help you get back on track when you have strayed.

Be observant of the other players at the jam. Is there is a player you really like but they don't seem to want to actively help you? Analyze their stage presence. What are they doing from the minute they walk on stage until they finish their last tune and walk off? How do they interact with the audience? How do they interact with the other players? What aspects of this do you like? What parts do you want to incorporate into your performance style? You can learn a great deal from examining their work without them coaching you on yours.

Also, look at their behavior off stage. Do they say hello to people? Are they friendly? This is a social gathering. Are they being social and interacting with other players in the scene? What are the differences between the player that is friendly and the player that isn't?

A jam is a place to network, meet other musicians on the scene, and have some fun. It is an opportunity to play with players you might not get a chance to play with under usual gig circumstances. A jam is a place to try to pick up some gigs. Subbing for other players on their gigs is a good way to work into a gigging scene. Those connections can often be made through networking at jams. Jams can also help you build an audience. Jams attract listeners that don't play an instrument. They may like that style of music or know a person that will be performing that evening. If they take a liking to your playing they might put in the effort to come to one of your performances.

Performing on stage is a demanding experience that requires you to pay attention and stay engaged with the music and musicians. Actively listening to the other players and reacting to their playing is important. If you've ever practiced with a Jamey Aebersold book or the iReal app you know the players on the track aren't going to respond to a musical idea you have developed. You don't want to give that type of performance to the other players you're performing with. A jam is supposed to be spontaneous. It typically isn't rehearsed. You have to react in real-time. Keep this in mind when you are playing. Interact musically with the other players on stage.

If you are a vocalist or instrumentalist outside of the rhythm section you will spend the time resting when others are soloing. Sometimes you may play a backing cue or pad behind a soloist but not continuously. You must stay engaged, know where you are in the form, and keep an eye on who is soloing and who still wants to solo so you can come back in with the melody at the appropriate time. If you are tuned out, the audience can tell. Your interactions with the other players will tell the story. Chances are you will miss your entrance or a cue to what is coming.

If you are in the rhythm section you will likely play the whole time. It is your job to make each passing chorus of the tune interesting. You must stay engaged and interact with the other players. If you go into an autopilot mode where you are not responding to the music you are making with others, that will take away from the performance. If there are many soloists, you may end up playing the piece for 10 minutes. Keep it interesting for yourself and others by being present and in the moment.

Above all else, enjoy the process.

Answers to playing examples of specific illustrations

Illustration 19 Answer: Started in measure 5
Illustration 20 Answer: Started in measure 9
Illustration 21 Answer: Started in measure 11
Illustration 22 Answer: Started at second A, half way through
Illustration 23 Answer: Started with last 6 measures, from the IV7
Illustration 24 Answer: Started at bridge

Sign-Up List

NAME	INSTRUMENT